This book contains personal experiences and spontaneous expressions excerpted from hundreds of unprepared presentations. They have been minimally edited to protect the innocent perfection that only life can create.

I hope they will touch you as deeply as they touched me the first time they traversed my awareness. These words did not come from me, they came THROUGH me in moments of emptiness.

– JACOB LIBERMAN
February 2001

Acknowledgments

Thank you to all the individuals who have continually reflected to me the next step of my journey:

My parents, Joseph and Sonia, and my sister and brother-in-law, Eva and Herb, for modeling real love and truth at a time when these qualities are often forgotten in our fast-moving world.

My children, Gina and Erik, for their friendship, love, and incredible clarity. Representing the next generation, their lives mirror to me the evolution of a new consciousness.

My wife and life partner, Claudia, for her bright light and unyielding commitment to her own development, and to the development of our union.

My friend and co-worker, Coleen d'Avignon, and her husband Pierre, for their support and daily reminders that I am on the right track.

My friends Denise Brugman, Sonja Langley, and Rose Brandt, for their loving assistance in initially transcribing and distilling the words that comprise the heart of this book.

My friend Paul Lowe, for taking me under his wing and helping me remember how to fly.

An extra-special thank you to my son Erik, for his countless hours of dedication to this project, and for his unique ability to allow the original message contained in these words to flow through him onto the page.

— JACOB LIBERMAN

Thank you to my father, who told me as we worked, "I am one source of your manifestation, and you are one creation of my vision. Together, we are two sides of the same coin." You gave me eyes to see, and encouraged me to use them. You are a light in my life, and I love you.

Thank you to my mother Marsha, my sister Gina, my aunts and uncles and my grandparents (especially Grandma Sonia, the first writer in the family) for their boundless love and support.

Thank you to my friends and teachers, Hank Berrings, Donald Eaholtz, Candida Condor, Caron Tate, Jenna Robinson, and Natalie Gold, for reminding me to find my "yes," even when everyone else said "no."

I dedicate this book to my future son, whom I see clearly before me. May we share as rich and wondrous time together as I've shared with my father.

— ERIK LIBERMAN

Wisdom has no author...
it comes through us anonymously.

Existence communicates its laws through nature and all its inhabitants. When we allow this heavenly communication to express itself through *our emptiness*, we disappear as separate personalities and become an indescribable radiance — Godliness itself. All that we cannot describe, we become instantaneously.

How It All Started

Twenty years ago, I was asked to give a one-hour presentation to a group of graduate students at a Florida university. I spent hours preparing my speech and made notes on about forty index cards.

As I walked to the podium on the day of my speech, I had a realization: I had perfectly prepared every sentence of a lecture about a subject I was supposedly an expert on!

Why had I prepared to talk about something I knew so well? I recognized in that moment that as far back as I could remember, my life had been a series of rehearsed announcements—an attempt to "look good," be accepted, and appear successful.

This realization was so shocking that my hand opened, allowing my perfectly prepared speech to fall all over the floor! It happened so fast that I had no time to pick up the cards—so I just stepped behind the podium and tried to collect myself.

After what seemed like an eternity, I took a deep breath and shared with the audience what had happened.

Without a moment's pause, the entire group and I sighed in unison as if the weight of the world had been lifted from our shoulders.

My one-hour presentation on learning disabilities turned into a three-hour informal discussion about learning without effort. I was never so unprepared for the miracle that occurred that day! I learned that I never had to prepare anything again, as long as I shared *only what I knew by heart*.

Now whenever I speak in public, I show up empty-handed and allow life to guide my expression. In the process, I've discovered that true wisdom has nothing to do with us, but with *how much of us is not there*.

The more present we become,
the more life communicates through us.

True wisdom
lies in not knowing.

Jumping In

I didn't think I was smart most of my life, and though I tried very hard, school was never easy for me. I didn't read much, and thought for sure that meant I was stupid.

When I got to college, I did everything I knew how to do to get into a professional school. After all, who would think someone with a doctorate was dumb? I needed some way of proving to others that I "knew something," even though I didn't feel very smart.

I earned degrees, made money, bought the house that I wanted and drove a fancy car, but life still felt empty. It was still a mystery! When I finally realized that wisdom had nothing to do with the degrees I had earned, I gave away all my books, notes, and research, packed away my diplomas, and set off to discover who I really was.

I showed up for life every day without preparation, even though I felt like I was doing the wrong thing over and over again. Even though I was frightened and felt like I was falling apart, I kept coming back. In having the courage to jump into life—not knowing if I would succeed—I grew.

You cannot see
a new point of view
from an old one.

Perspective

Imagine there are one hundred people, each standing on different floors inside the Empire State Building. When the person on the bottom floor looks out as far as they can, they may only see a few blocks away. That is their present view of reality, and anything beyond that, you might say is "the future."

The person on the second floor, because they are a little higher, may see a bit farther—their "present" is the future for those below them. With each successive floor, the observer's view expands. Thus, the person's view on top of the building—all the way to New Jersey!—is not even within the field of possibility for those on the lowest floors.

This is how awareness functions. We believe that we all see the same things, and often cannot imagine how others interpret things so differently. In reality, however, we all see things from our own perspective—or as the Talmud states, "We don't see things as they are. We see them *as we are.*"

When the "I" stops looking,
the eyes start seeing.

Seeing Holographically

Suppose for a moment that you don't see with your physical eyes—that you have no single "point of view," but can see clearly from all places at once. While meditating twenty-five years ago, I actually slipped into this indescribable state — and experienced a miraculous change in my vision.

Although my eyes were closed, *I could "see" myself sitting there in meditation*—only I couldn't tell where I was seeing myself from! It was as if the room was filled with eyes, and I was looking through all of them.

When I finally opened my eyes, my vision had undergone a profound change—from barely being able to see the eye chart, to seeing better than normal—and it has remained so to this day. Since I was a practicing optometrist at the time this shift occurred, it forced me to reconsider everything I had ever been taught about vision.

I realized that it is our *insight,* and not our eyesight, that must be healed if we wish to see clearly—and that only by *seeing beyond our beliefs* can we truly change our vision.

Seeing is not believing ...

Believing Is Seeing!

Once in Seattle, I gave an evening talk as part of a week-end workshop on vision. The next morning, I asked if anyone had experienced anything unusual during the night.

One participant replied, "I have been wearing contact lenses for twenty-six years. When I woke up this morning and opened my eyes, everything was blurry—like it always is before I put in my lenses.

"Then I looked at the ceiling, blinked, *and suddenly realized I hadn't taken out my lenses the night before.* At that moment, my vision cleared!"

True vision
is allowing the invisible
to become visible.

Satori

In the West, we think we see with two eyes, but in the East they have always been aware of a third eye, "the eye of contemplation," that looks within to see God. Let me share with you the difference an eye can make.

Place a hand over one of your eyes, and pretend that you live in a world where everyone has one of their eyes occluded. Look around the room for a moment. How does the world look from a one-eyed perspective? How does this one-eyed view of reality affect your feelings and beliefs?

Now, imagine that one day you're inspired to uncover this eye. Slowly raise your hand and notice your surroundings again. Outwardly, things look the same as before—the door is in the same place, the furnishings are the same color—yet seeing in this new way *feels* completely different.

You have just expanded your field of awareness from one eye to two eyes ... But what if we really have *three eyes,* and uncovering this third eye is the key to awakening our true vision?

In the East, they call such an awakening a *satori,* or "kick in the eye," and they say it is the way home.

The Light of God

Jonathon Swift wrote that real vision is the ability to see the invisible. In the past, the process of *how we create our lives* was only visible to a few enlightened mystics. As our awareness has expanded, however, more of us are now able to see what was once invisible to us.

For example, what we call "heaven" and "hell"—and thought was an after-life experience—we now see that we create *right here on earth,* by the way we live in each moment.

We are even beginning to recognize that we are not the physical body we so closely identify with, *but the visionary Source creating and animating it.*

Most of us experience this Source only when we have spiritual awakenings or near-death experiences. During these times, the body and chattering mind temporarily disappear, and only awareness remains.

What is awareness? It is not the individual "I" that we associate with the body, but the omniscient Seer within us—often referred to as God—which the Bible says is Light.

People who have had near-death experiences often describe entering a tunnel of light, not realizing that, as pure awareness, *they are the light they attempt to describe.*

Soon we will see that we not only come from light and return to it, but in between this coming and going, *we are always the same pure awareness called Light.*

Light is the invisible that illumines all that is visible.

*Creation is an outpouring
of inner vision.*

What You See Is What You Get

Physicist David Bohm said, "All matter is frozen light," meaning that light and life are the same essence in two different states of existence. One is the formless, spiritual Light we call God, and the other is the transformed expression of that Godliness we call life.

So, how does light become life? How does form-lessness miraculously alchemize into form? Quantum physics states that nothing exists without an observer, and the observer's point of view determines what is observed. In other words, *what we see* (in the mind) is *what we get* ("out there" in the world)!

We create *our experience of life* from what we believe is real or unreal, and what we create is no accident. It is our highest intelligence — our Godliness — mirroring back to us experiences that will expand our awareness and bring our consciousness to the next level.

Many people believe that Creation ended with the book of Genesis, but in fact it is constantly occurring. Creation never ends. It is God's "mind field," continually expressing itself as the heavens, earth, sun, moon, stars, and everything else that exists.

When things no longer matter,
life once again becomes light.

The Mind Makes It Matter

Just as the film in a projector transforms light into the movie we observe on the screen, the ideas imprinted in the mind convert the one light of Source into the rainbow of frequencies we experience as life. As we look at the world around us, we see a multicolored projection of our inner self. The frequencies of life we are attracted to represent the aspects of ourselves we are most comfortable with. The frequencies we are not attracted to remind us of the aspects of ourselves we've yet to embrace.

Change our ideas—the mind's film—and everything changes. When we stop identifying with our ideas altogether, the film dissolves completely, allowing light to move through us without resistance. We become full-spectrum beings—holographic focal points of the sun—radiating the light of God into the world.

When you pretend you can't
see what's in front of you,
you teach your eyes
to blur it out.

To See or Not to See

How often do we deny what we see to avoid discomfort? What would happen if we acknowledged everything we saw, heard, and felt?

When I became aware of how often I *pretended not to see* certain things, I began an around-the-clock practice. It went like this: Anything that entered my awareness became my responsibility, anything that was my responsibility I would be present with, and anything I was present with I would complete.

I practiced this for a week and didn't let anything get by me. By the end of the week, I was even picking up cigarette butts off the street! Now, twenty-five years later, seeing fully is an integral part of my nature.

There are many ways we can support the expansion of consciousness. However, I believe that simply *attending to whatever enters our awareness* is the most valuable practice we have for self-development. Our real insights come from the everyday work of being present—in our personal relationships, the way we run our businesses, and in honoring our commitments.

When we open our eyes to everything that touches us, we practice the highest level of vision.

When we stop looking for life,
it starts looking for us.

Stop Looking and Start Seeing

Observing an artist at work one day, I noticed that he periodically stepped back and gazed at his canvas. I wondered what he was looking at, until I realized he wasn't looking *at* anything in particular. He was simply opening his focus, softening his gaze, and allowing his vision to scan the work as a whole. Not looking for any one thing, his eyes were automatically drawn to whatever needed his attention in the painting.

After years of integrating this way of seeing into my own life, I've discovered that *in looking for nothing, we begin to see everything.* In fact, anything that requires our attention in life actually *finds us* when we stop looking for it. Living this way, we never have to "figure things out," or wonder "what to do next," because life keeps greeting us with the next step of our journey.

Forget spiritual mastery.
Master being human
and you'll get to the same place.

Living in the Moment

We often talk about "wanting to be spiritual," but being spiritual and taking care of our everyday affairs are exactly the same thing. There is no difference. *With clarity we become ordinary*—simply taking care of whatever comes before us. In this process, we develop trust that whatever shows up in our lives, we will meet it.

When we don't take care of things in the moment, they get backed up and we feel overwhelmed. But life never brings us anything at the wrong time! That's why everything in nature works so miraculously. Notice how the tides move, the earth rotates, and the trees grow. Notice how everything is perfectly timed—how our bodies work, how a child develops. God never makes a mistake.

So, when something enters our awareness, that's the moment to take care of it. Don't pay that bill tomorrow, take out the trash later, or make the bed when you get back. When you see it, do it! Don't prioritize anything— life has already done that for you.

Take care of what's in front of you,
and the universe will take care of you.

Human Beings

Imagine that life is simply about taking care of ourselves. Feeding ourselves, bathing ourselves, tending to whatever comes before us, and in that way, just *being*.

For most of us, the being side of life is underused, and the doing side is weighted down. When we are being, we are humane and very much in touch with everything in life. When we are doing, we forget the essence of our humanity and narrowly focus our minds on "making things happen." We forget that everything in life is already happening!

Our lives today are complex because we have lost sight of what is essential. We've developed technologies to handle the complexities we have created, but still have no time for living!

Living successfully isn't about making a lot of money. It *is* about embracing life, and responding to it honestly in each moment. This alone is the true source of our prosperity, because in this practice, we evolve from human doings to human beings.

When I do less, more things happen.
When I do nothing, everything happens.

Non-Doing

In the East, there is a state between doing and being called *wu-we-wu,* or *action without action.* I call it "non-doing." When I speak of non-doing, most people don't know what I'm talking about. They think I mean "laying back" and "hanging out"—a lethargic lifestyle.

But non-doing is not the opposite of doing! It is neither passive nor active, but a state of optimal presence and sensitivity. It is a fluid response to life, rather than a branding iron applied to life to get it to move "our way."

Competitive athletes refer to non-doing as "the zone." In this state, an appropriate response to any situation originates from our core and is not edited by the intellect. It defines *response-ability,* rather than *react-ability.*

Non-doing happens when we trust that life always has the first move—that in reality, we *are* living in a state of "not knowing"—and therefore, our actions are not isolated initiations based on our own desires, but responses to life's invitations.

Non-doing means that we are ready to respond to whatever life brings us, yet feel no need to initiate anything. It is the exquisite experience of being guided effortlessly and surprised by the miracle called life.

Animals live in the Kingdom of God.
We occasionally visit on weekends.

Being Normal Isn't Natural

Many of us pride ourselves on being "normal," but what we call normal may *not* be very natural—let alone healthy! If you're "normal," you will probably experience cancer, arthritis, vision loss, or heart disease sometime during your life, and your natural process of *saging* will be reduced to aging.

If you want to view life in its natural state, go into nature and observe animals. Wild animals live effortlessly in the Kingdom of God. They are always present —never doing anything early or late, excessively or deficiently. Their behavior is a model of the word "responsibility," meaning they respond to life with presence and awareness at all times.

When they're hungry, they eat. When they're not hungry, they don't worry about where their next meal will come from. You never see a bear looking for a job, doing aerobics, or taking a cigarette break! We are the only species with concepts of unemployment, exercise, and addiction.

In order to reclaim our natural connection with life, we must begin living with greater presence, respect, and gratefulness. We have been living under the illusion that evolution has ended with us at its helm. Perhaps the dinosaurs thought that, too!

Stop looking at the movie of life
one frame at a time,
and start seeing "the big picture."

The Movie of Life

When you watch a sad movie and your heart is touched, your eyes may fill with tears. When you watch an action movie, your adrenaline may rise and your pulse may race. Either way, you know you're not that person on the screen—you're just watching the movie.

Now, take that same movie, project it onto a 360-degree screen in Surround Sound, and place it inside your head. *That's the human mind.* Once you're in the mind, notice how quickly you forget who you are. How quickly you become convinced that you're the sum of everything on the mind's screen—thoughts, perceptions, and experiences—*rather than a timeless observer.*

Thoughts traverse our awareness like clouds across the sky. We forget, however, that *we're not the clouds—* we are the sky that remains clear and unchanging. When you realize that you're not the constantly changing scenery of the mind, you have discovered the essence of your true self.

Your true self is the observer. It has no thoughts, personality, or gender. It simply observes.

We speak of self-realization,
but when we realize,
there is no self.

Not the Individual "I," But the "I Am"

We believe we are our personality. But the essential self has no personality. All our habits, behaviors, and emotional issues are a facade resting over our essential self.

Our true nature is concealed by the names and labels we attach to it. When we say we are rich, poor, happy, or sad, who is this "we" we are talking about? Who would "we" be without any labels?

We are afraid that if we drop our personality, we will be left with nothing, or at least nothing that we recognize as ourselves. It's true—when we drop *our ideas* of who we are, we disappear as individual identities and instantly become everything—like drops of water falling onto the ocean.

Each time we identify with our essential self rather than our personality, we press the "Reset" button on our lives. Our mind's slate is wiped clean and we start again.

The essential self
cannot be described.
It is eternal.
It is infinite.
It is God.

Disappearing

Close your eyes. Notice your body—its heartbeat, breath, and posture. Notice your mind—its thoughts, beliefs, and judgments. Now notice *who is noticing*. That's the real you—the essential self.

The more we identify with the essential self, the more "we" disappear—not only our personality and beliefs, but even our physical form becomes more transparent and luminous. As our individual identity starts to dissolve, we begin to melt into the background, and our life transmutes back into light.

When people reach this state of being, they're usually not sitting and speaking to large groups. They may be raking leaves, or working in the garden. There is nothing "special" about them, yet we long to be around them because their presence awakens the Divinity within all of us. *Their life is their message.*

*Wellness is based
on how we live
in each moment.*

Being Whole

Like a body of water, life always seeks its own level. This ebb and flow, known to Chinese sages as yin and yang, is expressed in the field of health and wellness by the premise, "The body is always seeking homeostasis." In other words, the body is self-healing. Health, wholeness, and sanity are all expressions of this dynamic state of balance.

Most people today have forgotten this, however, and are looking for something or someone to "fix them." In fact, most traditional methods of healing are based on this approach.

The new vision of wellness must include everything we currently understand, yet look beyond techniques and treatments to the true source of healing and wholeness: presence.

With presence, we come into balance by *merely being*, and *not interfering* with life's natural self-healing ability. With presence, our every move is guided in an infinite process interconnecting and harmonizing all of life.

Change is constant
until you label it.

A Watched Pot Never Boils

One of the fundamental laws of quantum physics is that nothing changes while you're looking at it—a watched pot never boils. You can take a subatomic particle, put it into an unstable state, and as long as you are observing it, it will not change. In the East, they say that the appearance of things changes only when God is blinking.

For years I have said "It's not the disease that kills you, it's the diagnosis!" The moment we label anything, we stop its natural process of change. We are on a journey where nothing is fixed, but when we label something, we lock it into place.

We think we need to "work on things" in order to change them, but change is continuous. If you're "trying to change," you're actually swimming *against* the flow of life! Change is the essence of life. We notice it most when we look for it least.

Instant Healing

One Saturday afternoon, I had an impulse to check my throat in the mirror. I opened wide, and in the back of my throat I saw what appeared to be a brown growth I had never noticed before. My mind instantly went back twenty-five years, when my father was diagnosed with a cancerous growth in his throat.

I kept checking my throat, and every time I looked, the brown growth seemed larger. My heart rate accelerated, my blood pressure elevated, and my head and brow were drenched in sweat. My arms and legs turned cold, and I had a sudden attack of diarrhea.

The moment before, I was living in bliss, and now I was dying. My mind filled with the scenario I had always feared. Tomorrow—Sunday—I would be in the hospital, receiving the fatal diagnosis. By Monday my life would be over, and everything I had worked for would be meaningless.

After dwelling on this for a while, I picked up the phone and called a doctor friend. He asked, "What's wrong?"

"Stephen, I'm terrified. Both of my parents had cancer when I was a kid."

"I don't understand—what's the problem?"

"My parents are both alive and healthy now, but cancer has always been scary for me, because we never spoke about it openly."

"I still don't understand what's wrong."

"Well, I looked in the mirror this afternoon, and there was a brown growth in the back of my throat. It looks like a mole or something."

He asked me a few more questions, then told me to feel the bump with my finger. When I finally managed to squeeze my hand back there and pull it out, on the tip of my finger I found a little piece of the chocolate macaroon I had eaten for lunch.

Is there heaven or hell,
or do we just create them with the mind?

You Are What You Think

After going through a traumatic separation and divorce in the late 1970s, I fell apart. For eight years my life was a struggle, as I experienced thirty to forty massive anxiety attacks a day. Sometimes I was so frightened, I didn't know if I would survive. My world view dissolved in front of my eyes, and it seemed like every time I had a thought, it instantly translated into a bodily sensation—as if my mind and body were one.

Now, more than twenty years later, it is scientifically known that every state of mind *we identify with* manifests as a chemical messenger, telling the body what to do, when to do it, and to what degree. These "molecules of emotion" not only guide the body's biological functions, but also alert everybody around us as to what our body is feeling and thinking.

The degree to which the mind influences the body, however, is determined by *how much we identify with its chatter*. In other words, are we the thinker of our thoughts, or the one noticing the thoughts? Only in recognizing that *we are the noticer* and not the thinker, can we stop interfering with life's natural flow towards health and wellness on every level.

Our ideas determine how we see—not only molding our physical eyesight and mental outlook, but the way our entire body works. The same constriction in our view of reality also constricts our kidneys, our heart, our liver, and our blood vessels. So when we talk about "expanding consciousness," that expansion supports every organ in our body, as well as every thing in the universe!

Your body is the living canvas of your thoughts.

The heart of healing
is the healing of the heart.

Wellness Is Contagious

One of the most interesting scientific findings in the last few years is that there is no way of separating the experimenter from the experiment. This is not a new idea. In the East they say that the seer and the seen are one—that we are all inseparably connected in a Divine relationship.

Now, imagine how this discovery might affect the relationship between a doctor and their patient. Could a doctor's limiting beliefs about reversing a certain condition actually inhibit their patient's ability to do so? How might it affect a patient if their healing practitioner believed in miracles? As science opens its eyes to what mystics have always seen, can we let go of the ideas and beliefs that limit the infinite possibilities within our life's experience?

Doctors of the future will be teachers of wholeness who exemplify what it means to be human—by relating more and repairing less. Health is no longer an issue of merely repairing broken parts, but of mending broken hearts.

The degree to which we are
real, ordinary human beings,
is the degree to which we influence others.

Mensch

During a workshop in Switzerland, one of the participants began to share about her life. As she spoke, it became apparent that she was very angry with the men in her life, and that she projected that anger onto all men. Almost every sentence began with "Men are ..." or "Men always..."

Since she trusted me, I asked if she would share with the group her first response to a question I had. She closed her eyes and I asked her, "Am I a man or a woman?" She paused for a moment, then answered, "You're a mensch."

In German, *mensch* means human being. In Yiddish, however, when someone says "You're a mensch," it means that you define what it means to be human, to be humane. To be a mensch is to be sensitive, loving, and caring. It speaks of a quality irrespective of gender, race, religion, or any of the other ways we separate ourselves from the oneness of life.

Rather than being a man or woman, black or white, Jewish or Christian, consider just being a mensch.

The ultimate meditation
is being here now...
eyes open, present, and responsive.

Crisis Leads to Opportunity

Getting upset is not a problem, it's a solution. It's the point from which we can expand—a natural launching pad for our growth and development.

To take full advantage of this process, we must become aware of the aspects of life that trigger our upset, then use these experiences as opportunities to practice the art of being present.

Being present doesn't mean that you never worry or get angry. It means that you are present *with* your worry and your anger. Whether you're laughing or in a funk, don't suppress it, process it, or project it onto someone else.

Instead, remain present with whatever arises, allowing your awareness to distill and transform it appropriately. In the process, you'll become free.

Do we ever really change,
or do we simply learn to accept
the person we've always been?

Coming Home

Many people believe that meditating, "eating right," or following a specific spiritual path will lead to a state of enlightenment.

For me, however, "enlightenment" is recognizing that there is nothing to do, nowhere to go, and no one to become. It's about being who you are, however you are, in each moment.

We've all been conditioned to believe that we were born with missing pieces. We spend our lives trying to become *who we think we would have been* were all our pieces intact. But nothing has been lost! The person we are looking for is the same one who started on the journey — *we already are the person we're trying to become.*

When we see this, we stop "chasing our tail," and life gets much simpler! We drop into this moment with *our presence,* and come home.

When life becomes our meditation,
we experience heaven on earth.

Meditation

When I was first introduced to meditation, I would practice twice a day for twenty minutes. Sometimes I used a mantra; other times I switched between watching my breath, focusing on the third eye, or touching the roof of my mouth with my tongue. It all seemed to work while I was meditating, but shortly thereafter I found myself back in the "real world," unable to maintain the same peace inside. So I tried something different.

My new practice consisted of watching my breath during 20 one-minute meditations daily. I then modified it to 40 thirty-second meditations, and eventually to 80 fifteen-second meditations a day. After a while, I even began practicing with my eyes open while driving my car or eating. I felt such a wonderful release each time I did it that I started watching my breath as often as I could.

Initially, it might only last for the moment it took me to drive to the end of the block. Then I would extend it, watching my breath until I got to the traffic light three blocks away. Eventually those short intervals connected for extended periods and the outside world began to disappear. I was aware of everything, but there was nothing "out there." As my mind emptied, the world emptied, and heaven and earth merged into one.

The best way to preserve
a child's vision
is to let them see things their way
rather than yours.

Adulteration

We have forgotten the secret of life. We knew it as children because we didn't "do" anything as children, we simply enjoyed ourselves, responding to life as it called to us. We never asked one another, "What do you do?" or "What do you wanna be when you grow up?" Those were questions adults asked.

Growing up, we became "adulterated," forgetting that life was supposed to be fun—an experience of learning through living! Everything became serious. We had to go to school and earn degrees. We had to "become someone" and "be successful." In the process, we learned to be successful at everything *except life*. We forgot the magic of simple, ordinary, uncomplicated living!

As a Whole, or Through a Hole

Early in life, before we knew we were anything or anyone, before we saw ourselves as separate from others, we lived in bliss.

This blissful spell was broken when we first experienced ourselves *as a reflection of how others saw us.* This distorted image was in such opposition to the fullness we initially experienced that it dispelled our state of wholeness, and replaced it with a field full of holes.

The innate wisdom that guided us through life initially was supplanted by an identity that *thought first,* then carefully maneuvered through the "mind field" it had created. Over time, our "personality" emerged as the compensatory behaviors we identified with, while our essence went underground, waiting for the right moment to resurface.

Like a flower blooming in the light of day, our essential nature is always yearning to expand and express its fragrance. It is the driving force behind our evolution, continually creating experiences that reflect to us who we really are.

Like two trains moving towards each other, we continually *run into ourselves*, "cracking the egg" that holds the form of our personality, and revealing to us our infinite wholeness.

To experience the essential self,
we have to see life as a whole,
rather than through a hole.

*Meet life with the curiosity of a child
and the perseverance of an adult.*

The Terrible Two's

As a child approaches the age of two, it naturally begins to individuate from its parents. Most parents are not quite ready for that, however. They truly believe their children are "theirs." *We do not realize that life cannot be held, only appreciated!* The moment we think we have ownership over anything, that "thing" begins to pull away from our grasp.

When a child begins walking, let it walk. If you continue to pick it up when it doesn't want to be held, it feels violated so it pulls away. Of course there is concern about the child's welfare—you don't want it to get hurt, so you need to set up a space where it can exercise its new skills and not get injured. That is not the real issue, however.

The real issue is that when children begin following their own guidance rather than the artificial rules we have set up, they remind us of the fun and freedom we aren't having—and of the innocence and purity of our inner nature.

So what are the terrible two's? That's the time when our children begin standing on their own "two feet," reminding us of the life we were meant to live.

*Life always serves us
the exact curriculum we need ...
It may not be what we want,
but it is always what we need!*

Changing the Subject

When I was a child, my father and I used to clash a lot, and sometimes it got pretty heated. When it got too loud for my mother, she'd turn to my dad and say, "Joe, can't we just change the subject?"

We're all addicted to changing the subject—changing the channel on life. But life isn't a television set, and we aren't here to channel surf.

Addictions such as drugs, alcohol, and food are the most obvious ways of distracting ourselves. The *real* addiction, however, is in the habitual way we avoid being present with our life's curriculum, creating pain and suffering in the process.

If "what we resist, persists," then avoiding our life's work only perpetuates our suffering. Be here now—nothing else works.

Conditioning

Imagine being born into a family where most things are not expressed openly and, in general, everyone is "keeping it together." As children growing up in this environment, we might feel embarrassed sharing our feelings and tend to keep things inside.

When an emotional event occurs, we hold our breath, our throat closes down, and our lower back and pelvis hold on for dear life. We become tense, which is why our bodies are so elastic when we're children, yet tighten as we get older. Our beliefs grow more fixed, and our bodies and organs hold these ideas firmly in place.

Since life is self-healing, however, our highest intelligence keeps re-creating experiences to dislodge these feelings, allowing them to surface and be recycled into life. In instances where an object is left in a patient during surgery—such as a non-dissolving suture—it is not uncommon for the object to find its way out of the body years later at a different location. Just as a foreign object attempts to free itself from the body, an unexpressed emotion will try to dislodge itself from our consciousness any way it can.

We are a flow-through system where every experience simultaneously empties our past and nourishes our expansion in the present. Nothing in life is meant to be held, not even memories. As we become more present, our memories of the past are gradually replaced by an innocent curiosity for life, and once again we see through the eyes of a child.

*Life is always moving us
in the direction of expansion,
regardless of our choice.*

Thinking ahead
keeps us behind.

Cheating

As children, we were told that the ability to think was the crown jewel of evolution, and that humans were the most evolved creatures because we were the ones who could think. But isn't most of our thinking simply an attempt *to guarantee that things come out "our way"*? Isn't thinking just a fancy word for worrying? And aren't we worrying because we're afraid to be just who we are?

This worrying that we call thinking is really the most sophisticated form of *cheating* ever devised—but we are only cheating ourselves. Every time we rehearse life in the mind, we cheat ourselves of the opportunity to discover our true genius. We rob ourselves of the realization that, even when we don't think ahead, *life still brings us what we need.* Life requires no rehearsal, but we will never know that until we meet it without preparation.

We need to take a chance and be spontaneous every opportunity we have—feeling life rather than analyzing it, listening to our hearts rather than our minds. Only in living spontaneously does our life distill into its purest essence.

Keep sweeping things under the rug…
and sooner or later you'll trip and fall.

Your Life Depends On It

Children playing with matches occasionally burn their fingers. If, however, they learn of these dangers and *still* pretend they don't know what's going on, they're asking for big trouble. The same is true for parents who think that if they pretend everything is fine—even when it's not—their children won't notice. Then they wonder why their kids get so off-track in their lives, living in an environment that looks one way on the outside but feels totally different on the inside.

If you know that things aren't working in your life and you pretend that they are, you are creating problems for yourself. You may wonder why life has served you this meal, but eventually you'll realize that you cooked it up in your own kitchen!

When you are truly unaware, life is very forgiving. But when you know and pretend that you do not, you create consequences. You cannot be honest only when it is convenient. You cannot pretend that you see only when you want to. Your life requires 100% presence. You cannot afford to get off course. Your life depends on it.

There are no consequences
other than those we create.

You Can't Get Away With Anything

When I was thirteen years old, I sold newspapers after school on a street corner in Miami. I would walk between the cars stopped at a traffic signal and yell out, "Five-Star Final!" I earned a penny for each paper I sold. One day I got out of school late and had to go to work without eating a snack. I was hungry but hadn't earned any money yet, so I went into a store and stole a candy bar.

As I walked out feeling guilty, a voice inside my head said, "Nobody saw you." Suddenly I realized something amazing: *I saw me*!

My life changed that day when I realized *there is never anyone watching but ourselves*. We can never "get away" with anything, because we are all there is! Whatever we do, we do to ourselves—there is no one else.

When you begin to wake up,
you see how often you were asleep.

The Mirror of Life

Each time you forget that life is a reflection of your actions, you get a reminder. When it shows up, don't go into the mind searching for excuses—just be grateful and move on.

Imagine you're speeding down the road and a police officer pulls you over. Notice how your mind automatically comes up with all sorts of excuses and reasons for speeding. Have you considered that another vehicle may have been approaching at high speed just around the corner, and the officer may have just saved your life?

When you get the message, you rarely need the ticket. But when you don't get the message, you always get the ticket!

Seeing things as right or wrong
obscures the truth.

To Agree Or Disagree

When someone says something, we usually agree or disagree. If we agree, we elevate the other person because they have confirmed our point of view. If we disagree, we argue with them so that we don't feel the discomfort of surrendering our point of view.

But what if having *no point of view* is actually our ticket to freedom? What if having no point of view means neither agreeing nor disagreeing with anyone? What would life be like if we simply accepted everything we saw as *a fact,* rather than as a problem?

Consider a different approach in your life. Listen to what everyone says and don't agree or disagree. Just allow yourself to be touched, and see how it feels inside. You don't have to "figure it out." If there's something to what they said, embrace it. If nothing resonates, thank them and move on.

If you're trying hard
to get someone to understand something,
then you still don't understand.

Direct Experience

My friend shared about an incident that occurred when she lived in a secluded little cabin in the middle of a large field. One day she looked out her window and saw two people dressed in suits walking towards the cabin. She thought, "Well, they're either tax collectors or missionaries." They got to the cabin, and they were in fact missionaries.

She invited them in and they started to talk about Jesus. All of a sudden my friend said to them, "Well, do you think he looks like his pictures?" They looked at each other and didn't know what to say. Then she asked, "How will you know when Jesus comes? How will you know he is here if you don't know what he looks like?"

They were silent for a moment, said "Thank you," turned around, and walked out. In questioning how well they knew Jesus, my friend realized that they knew him more in their minds than from a direct heart experience.

If you believe something that is not your experience, you limit yourself. Neither believe nor disbelieve anything, just be present in each moment, *and the truth will make itself known to you.* Let life be your guide, and you will know everything by heart.

Once you discover the truth,
you can no longer lie.

The High Price of Manipulation

Imagine going into a bank, and the teller mistakenly gives us too much money. We notice something is wrong, yet say nothing. As soon as we get outside, we feel a bit funny. Life is giving us a second signal, but we just change the subject and keep going. As we walk down the block, once again we feel an uneasiness, pause for a moment, then ask ourselves, "Should I or shouldn't I?" We know what is going on, but continue walking. A little later while driving our car, we crash into the car in front of us—and suddenly the $40 we accidentally received from the teller costs us $4,000.

Whenever we "bend life our way," by avoiding the signals it gives us, we move *against the flow*—and that is very expensive in the long run. The more we avoid our "gut feelings," the more we create a need for life to give us a louder message.

When we're really present, however, there is no choice but to act in accordance with the guidance life provides us. We respond to life's *whispers,* implicitly trusting the intelligence of the universe.

*It's not your experience
that creates your complaint,
it's your complaint
that creates your experience.*

Complaint

Once during a workshop, my event coordinator invited me to take a walk around a lovely, duck-filled lake. Hundreds of people walked and jogged around the lake's perimeter, and as we spoke, I noticed that my companion was constantly complaining. It seemed as if his entire life was one big complaint!

We continued walking when I noticed a man nearby with a very large head and malformed appendages. His entire body—probably just two feet long—was strapped to a motorized wheelchair. To my amazement, he was working a little joystick and navigating himself around the course, keeping up with the other joggers. Suddenly, he looked up. We made eye contact, smiled, and it was love at first sight!

It was incredible. Here was one person with all of his faculties and no obvious problems constantly complaining, while another person with very obvious obstacles in his life had no complaints—only a smile. The man in the wheelchair, his long hair flying in the breeze, was having such a good time, and seemed so grateful to be alive!

We can all come to a place in our lives where our gratitude is so big, there is no room for anything else.

Meltdown

My son called me one night to share some things he was going through. As I listened, I noticed that whatever was going on for him was escalating. He got increasingly upset, and it was clear that he wanted me to "jump into the cesspool" with him. Nevertheless, I just remained present, and noticed as his energy got louder and louder. Finally he became angry and hung up the phone.

The next morning he called back and said, "Dad, you beautiful man."

I said, "Erik, what's going on?"

He said, "Well, last night I was really going through some stuff, and I didn't realize until afterwards how much I wanted to hook you in! I didn't like the place I was in, and I didn't want to be there alone. I wanted someone else to feel the way I did, but you didn't jump in, you just kept loving me. After I hung up, I realized that I was left with exactly what I came in with. It was like trying to climb a steel wall that had oil on it. I couldn't grab onto anything, so I was left with me. And as I sat there feeling the pain and frustration, something just melted down. Thanks. I love you."

This is what happens when we no longer engage with someone who is triggered about something. It's not about knowing how to defuse a situation when someone is angry. It *is* about noticing how, with presence, the things that used to "hook us in" no longer do, and life's problems take care of themselves.

Misery loves company.
Bliss doesn't need any.

Life can never be "the way it used to be."
Evolution doesn't go backwards.

Past and Present

We are often told that the source of our problems lies in the past, and that if we want to change, we must uncover and understand "what happened." What we fail to realize is that every moment we spend in the past, we lose in the present! The part of us that "wants to understand" is also the part of us that doesn't want to change. It uses "understanding" to distract us from being present, where the only real change can occur.

Consider this: Rather than searching your memory for understanding, notice what you are doing *in this moment* to maintain the presence of your past experiences. Notice that each time you repeat those behaviors, you sign another year's lease on your old patterns.

When presence becomes your life's priority, however, the exact curriculum needed for transformation is revealed without thought or effort on your part. Old patterns find their own resolution, and you no longer relate to them in the same way. When you are truly present, the past and future dissolve into the here and now.

*Our stories are the glue
that keep our lives from changing.*

Stop Telling Stories

Everyone has stories about unpleasant things that have happened to them sometime in their life. In fact, we frequently identify with these stories. They could be about our childhood, a difficult divorce, or how someone has taken advantage of us. What we don't realize is that *these stories are killing us.* They are the albatross around our neck that doesn't allow us to move forward with our lives.

When we tell our story, we usually attract someone who likes to tell theirs. As they say, "Birds of a feather flock together." However, if we notice that we are in our story and *disengage,* we can abort mission midstream. As we begin to catch ourselves, *our awareness becomes curative.* With time, we naturally disconnect from our own stories and don't engage in anyone else's.

If we could just forget
who we think we are,
everything would change.

Forgetting Yourself

Imagine you are handed a special pill. You will take this pill before falling asleep tonight, and by the time you awaken in the morning you will have forgotten everything you have ever known.

When you look in the mirror, you won't remember who you are. You won't remember whether the image you see is "male" or "female." You won't remember your favorite foods. You won't remember if you can see clearly without your glasses, or if you are happy with your lover. It's even possible that when you look in the mirror, *no one will be there*.

If you took this pill and forgot yourself completely, if you had no preconceived ideas about yourself, who would be left? Would you still have the same ache or injury you had the day before? If you were diagnosed with some disease, would it still be there if you had no memory or concept of it?

What would happen if the next time you had a feeling, you had no labels or memories to make sense of it? What would you call this thing? Would you take particular notice of it in the first place—or would your "sense of self" simply be a passing sensation, emerging then dissolving back into the ocean of life?

*Breath is the source
of our inspiration.*

Breathe

Breath is an expression of our state of presence. When we are not present, we hold our breath, our awareness collapses, and we feel distant from life. When we are present, our breath fills, our awareness expands, and *life breathes us.*

Breath reflects our inward and outward relationship with life—our acceptance of the new and release of the old. When we are present, there is no break between inhalation and exhalation as we flow seamlessly with life, moment by moment.

We are all connected, and our every thought and intention is expressed in our breathing. Hold your breath, and everyone around you holds theirs. Allow life to breathe you, and the world breathes easier.

Thinking and Breathing

Have you ever noticed that while thinking, your breathing narrows? For most people, thinking causes them to hold their breath, because each thought stops life in its tracks.

When you notice the mind chattering away, a very simple thing to do is just tune into your breathing. Watch the body inflate and deflate with each breath. Within a short period of time, the mind quiets, and after a while your breathing changes as well.

Observe the breath, and you'll notice that it fills not only your upper lungs, but also expands into your diaphragm. Watch the breath some more, and you'll feel it deepen into the pelvic girdle, as if one is giving birth.

Become even more present, and you'll begin breathing inside your head, your legs, and then your entire body. When that happens, the breath rate drops dramatically

—from fifteen to five to three to two and eventually to one breath per minute.

The breath deepens, the mind quiets, everything slows down, and life gets fuller, longer, and richer. You're aware of the mind's chatter, but there's no attempt to shut it off. Even if you become an expert meditator, the mind still does what the mind does. However, in recognizing that the mind chatters just as the heart beats, we find a way of including it without attending to it.

When we think, the breath disappears.
When we breathe, the mind disappears.
Start breathing.

Most crises occur
when we step out of the moment
and into the mind.

Mind Fields

The automatic pilot on an airplane responds to present situations based on past programming. It deals with most situations fairly well, but introduce the unknown, and the high-tech autopilot is helpless.

The human mind works the same way. While it can be incredibly useful, *our total presence* must be at the helm of our lives, using the mind as a tool *when needed*. Most of us have forgotten this, however, so we live at the mercy of the mind's chatter.

When I become aware of the chatter in my own mind, rather than trying to suppress it, I *include* it in my life's experience without interacting with it. Eventually, the chatter quiets and feels increasingly distant—like a pair of audio speakers moving further and further away from me.

The less we interact with the mind's chatter, the more our awareness expands; *we* become bigger and the mind becomes smaller. Instead of *reacting* to life based on our past conditioning, we r*espond* to it as it shows up in each moment. The chatter that used to dominate our lives is then replaced by the silent hum of our natural intelligence.

The mind lies between you and life.
Without the mind, you are life.

The "I" or the "Eye"?

When we are present, we can experience both the small thinking mind—our intellect—and the large knowing Mind—our intelligence. The first is the mind of man, the second the Mind of God, and both dwell within us.

Through our intellect, we experience ourselves as individuals, separate from God and from life. Our ideas are exclusive, because we relate to life from an "I want it my way" point of view. This becomes evident when the side effects of our "technological advancements" outweigh the benefits.

When we experience life through our intelligence, however, we see from the heart, and recognize our connectedness with all of life. Our creations are *inclusive* and support everything, in no way disturbing nature's harmony.

Are we creating our lives from the "I" of the intellect, or the "eye" of intelligence? If we view ourselves as separate from life, our creations will further distance us from it. Let's not try to "fix" life with another good idea —life doesn't need fixing.

Creation

The Mind's desire initiates a wave of intention that results in creation. The purity of this level of creation has nothing to do with the intellect. It has to do with following life's invitations — the bigger thoughts — which are not thoughts we think, but *thoughts that think us*.

Each time we follow life's invitations, we become more sensitive to its callings, and develop trust. Not trust in anything specific, just trust in life. The process resembles a target, where ideas originating from the Source traverse our awareness, effortlessly hitting the bull's eye of life without interference from the intellect. In other words, *life lives itself through us, when we stay out of the way*.

Most people's experience of creation is radically different than this, however. They experience life's invitations through their intuition, but rarely follow them. Perhaps if we were more present, we would notice the continual revelations entering our awareness meant to guide us through life effortlessly. Instead, most of us follow our intellect's ideas, constantly replacing what we feel in our hearts with what we see in our heads.

Genesis tells us that at the end of each day of Creation, "God saw that it was good." Kabbalic scholars interpret this as meaning that *God's seeing actually resulted in creation.* In other words, subjective reality preceded objective reality. The Talmud states, "We do not see things as they are. We see them as we are." The essence of creation has not changed since Biblical times! In not interfering with the Divine essence continually expressing itself through us, our lives become a miraculous extension of God's creation.

When intention and attention are aligned, the archer and target become one.

Slow down,
you missed your life.

What's the Rush?

Have you noticed how everyone is constantly on the run? What are they running to—or, more appropriately, *running from*? Sometimes when I'm in a big city, I cannot accelerate fast enough from a traffic signal to avoid someone honking their horn as a way of saying "Hurry up!" Why is everyone in such a hurry?

Today while driving, I slowed down for a pigeon in the road. In that moment, I realized that the pigeon was no different than a person crossing the street. So often our connectedness with life goes out the window when we are in a rush. Are there really any emergencies in life, or do we create them by living as though we are always in the midst of one?

Perhaps new cars should be equipped with biofeedback equipment giving us continuous readings on our stress levels. I wonder how fast we would move if we realized that *our lives are being shortened by our rushing.*

Just as the speed of a race car determines how fast it reaches the finish line, our speed also governs how quickly we reach our finish line. How quickly would you like to be finished?

A Near-Life Experience

I once had a "near-death experience." I was reminded of it recently while eating a bowl of lentil soup. As I lifted the spoon, my eye fell on a large bay leaf, and instantly I was back in 1979 in the dining room of the Mutiny Hotel in Miami. They had a dinner show, and their specialty was French onion soup with lots of cheese, which I really loved.

Without looking, I took a big spoonful of cheese and swallowed it. I didn't notice the large bay leaf embedded in it, but immediately I knew something was wrong. One moment I was enjoying the show; the next moment I was lying on the floor, gasping for air. The room was dark, and all of the other diners were focused on the performance.

In an instant, my entire life passed through my awareness at the same speed I had originally experienced it. I didn't miss a detail. I saw everything I had ever felt, *and everything anyone else had ever felt in response to me.* Nothing was rushed, yet it all took less than a few seconds.

Before I knew it, a doctor at the next table did the Heimlich maneuver on me and forced the food out of my windpipe.

How was it possible for me to review my entire life at normal speed within a few seconds? Yet ask anyone who has ever had a near-death experience, and they'll tell you the same thing: Every detail of your life flashes before you — not just your actions, but the consequences of your actions, spreading through the vast network of everyone who has ever been touched by your existence.

Why wait for a near-death experience to realize the impact that everything you do has on everything that exists?

Your every intention, thought, and action touches all of existence.

"No Body" Does Not Mean Nobody

Consider this: You go out on the ocean in a small boat and all you see is the ocean. You sense there is something going on beneath the surface, but you have no direct contact with it. All of a sudden, a dolphin jumps into the air, and for a moment that dolphin is part of your reality—then it is gone.

Did the dolphin die when you could no longer see it? Then how can you be sure that *you die* when your body is no longer visible in this reality? We, like the dolphin, appear to jump in and out of this plane, but we are always here—though not always visible.

We speak of "leaving the body," but we never leave the body, nor do we enter it. *We merely infuse it with life's force and guide it through its intuitive senses.* You might say that we are the spiritual eyes and heart of the human energy system. Just as a lamp needs to be plugged into an electrical outlet to light up, our essential self is the Source of light in this body.

When the body dies, we don't die, we continue doing what we have always done—*infusing life with light*. We are the formless photons physicists speak of. We are the intelligence accessed when people have instantaneous healings and spiritual awakenings. We are the Source of love, inspiration, and vision—the thread connecting every thing.

*We are the Light
that creates, illuminates,
and animates the image
we call "us."*

Truth benefits everyone,
whether they know it or not.

Communication

There is an art to communication. It has to do with sharing *just what we are experiencing,* then listening to what the other person is experiencing. Rather than presuming to know what someone else is feeling and thinking, or arguing about who's right and who's wrong, communication starts by sharing our individual truths, *without interruption.*

Growing up, most of us did not have role models for how to relate in this way, and therefore find communication difficult. We bend over backwards trying to "make things work out" with others, which usually leads to resentment.

When we start sharing *just what we are experiencing,* our communication takes a quantum leap. We realize that our experience is happening within ourselves, and is just that—*our experience.*

We share our feelings, the other person shares their feelings, everything gets aired out, and while no one is looking, a whole new level of non-compromised truth emerges.

Kindness is cruel
if it compromises the truth.

Honest Expression

We need to communicate the same way a baby communicates. When it's hungry it lets you know. It's no more complicated than that, but we often turn truthful communication into an intellectual process.

Sometimes we say the truth is "hard and cold," but the only time it feels hard and cold is when it has been held back, compromised, or wrapped with false kindness. It's like putting a lid on a pressure cooker—the pressure builds and the lid wants to blow off!

In each moment, truth is just innocence. It is the next thing that enters our awareness. No more or less truthful than the expression that preceded it or the one that follows.

We have moved so far away from this level of communication that we end up having wars. First we compromise ourselves by not sharing our truth with another. Then we resent that "other" as a result of our own lack of communication. What started off as a battle within us leads to a war with another person, then another group, then another nation.

We all live in the same world, share the same heart, and have the same things going on inside us. Let's begin again.

Whenever love knocks on your door,
let it in.

Without Intimacy, We Experience Loss

Once I shared with a friend during a phone conversation that I had fallen in love with someone who lived on the other side of the world. He immediately remarked, "Geographically undesirable."

I replied, "What are you talking about?"

He said, "Couldn't you have chosen someone closer to home?"

But can we really choose where or when we connect with our soulmate?

Real love is so rare that if we are fortunate enough to experience it, we will be left speechless, floating in a sea of stillness so full that words cannot in any way capture its breadth. Love is like life. We don't choose when it comes and we don't choose when it goes. We simply appreciate it while it's here.

Things Either Work or They Don't

Have you noticed how much of our lives are spent trying to make certain relationships "work out"? From my experience, relationships either work or they don't! It's like falling in love: it either happens or it doesn't. When it happens there is nothing you can do about it, and when it doesn't happen there is nothing you can do about it.

That doesn't preclude the fact that there's a constant stream of relating within all relationships—but there must be a fundamental, ineffable bond of love that joins us in the first place.

Here's an example. I was doing an event in Austria, and my interpreter walked in. We made eye contact, and instantly connected without saying a word. I had worked with four different interpreters up to that point, but when this woman sat next to me, we were immediately drawn together. Our energies seamlessly merged in a dance so smooth that I wasn't sure whether she was interpreting me or I was interpreting her. The harmony of our connection melted both of us.

By the way, that woman and I were married four and a half months later, and to this day it is still love at first sight! And no matter how choppy the waves of life may be at times, it is clear that our love is as deep as the ocean.

Try rising into love,
rather than falling in it.

What keeps us up at night
is what we have kept down
during the day.

No Big Deal

It is rare that I ever see two people living together in bliss, yet I know it is possible if we are willing to live in total integrity. That means sharing from the depth of our being with truth, caring, and *no editing.*

The more present we become in our lives, the more we allow for this level of communication—and the greater our chances for experiencing bliss.

A friend once said to me, "When we don't say it, it's a big deal. When we say it, it's no big deal!" When we don't share something that *wants to be expressed,* we create a build-up of energy. When we allow life to flow through us *without resistance,* however, there is no build-up—it's no big deal. That's bliss!

Each time you compromise yourself,
you send out an invitation
for future resentment.

Compromise

When we get to the point in our lives where we are unwilling to compromise our truth, we will experience everything differently. However, we must first recognize *whether we are genuinely responding to our inner truth,* or doing something because it is the "right" thing to do.

For instance, if being a vegetarian is natural for us and supports our wellness, great. But if it is a "cause," or a way of rebelling against non-vegetarians, then it will not support our total health. In fact, our againstness may actually poison the benefits of "eating right."

I went out with my daughter Gina one night to a small local restaurant. At the time both of us were eating a vegetarian diet. While considering the menu, we suddenly looked up at each other and knew what the other was thinking. Without a pause we both said, "Let's do it!" She had the lamb chops and I had the filet mignon.

I had not eaten meat in fifteen years, and it was wonderful. I don't know if it was wonderful because it was wonderful, or because I didn't deny myself the experience I needed to have. All I know is that there is no longer any room in my life for compromise. I trust my inner guidance, and follow that guidance implicitly.

Save Room for Dessert

While having lunch with my daughter at a sidewalk cafe in Zurich, a man came up to our table and placed a card with a pen next to our plates. Not knowing who this man was, I could only guess that he was a waiter giving us the dessert menu.

As I looked at the card, I saw that it had four paragraphs all written in different languages. The bottom one was in English and read, "I cannot hear or speak, and I am not begging for money. I sell these pens to support myself so that I may live like everyone else."

Suddenly I realized that my first intuition was correct—this was the dessert menu! While the man walked around the restaurant placing his cards and pens on each of the tables, I reached into my pocket and pulled out twenty Swiss francs.

By the time I looked up, the restaurant manager had seen the man and started screaming at him to leave. The man turned his head lovingly towards me as if to ask, "What did I do?"

As he collected his cards and pens, I handed him the twenty francs. He smiled. I felt grateful. For the restaurant manager, this incident was hell. For me, it was heaven. We choose our heaven or hell in each moment. What will your next choice be?

*Life can be heaven or hell.
It's your choice.*

Spirit of Generosity

A few years ago, I gave a presentation at a healing conference in Egypt. One afternoon, I hired a guide with a camel to take me on a tour through a local village. I was very fortunate that my guide, an angelic little boy, took me through the village where he lived with his family. We rode through several narrow dirt roads, and I noticed that most of the families there were living in rooms the size of an average walk-in closet.

It was mid-afternoon and people were having their lunch. As we rode by, everyone we passed looked up and motioned for us to come down and eat with them. We must have passed sixty of these tiny shacks in just one block, and from every one, without exception, someone waved and invited us to join them. These people had no money, no toilets, and for the most part slept on the ground, yet every one of them had plenty of food to share.

Here, we live in a country with an abundance of everything. Yet when most of us sit down to eat, we act as if it's our last meal. There's a feeling of *exclusivity*. How often do we include all that is around us in our bounty? When I speak of including, I don't mean offering food or giving money as a means of being polite or generous. In fact, I am not talking about anything we *do*. I am referring to a spirit of generosity that comes from recognizing our connectedness with all of life.

When we are in touch with this unity, there is no difference between ourselves and the person begging on the street. We are one and the same.

If you want to experience prosperity,
start giving things away.

Give away what is not essential
and you will discover what is.

More Space In My Life

An elderly woman at one of my workshops asked if she should purchase one of the color therapy instruments we manufacture. I told her I thought the device might be helpful to her, but there was something about her spending the money for a new machine that didn't feel right to me.

I sat with it and remembered that someone had called my office a week or two earlier, wanting to sell a barely used device at a reduced price. I shared this with her, but something still felt unclear.

Later that day, I found a box in my garage. I thought it contained something of my son's, but when I opened it, there was a prototype of a color therapy device I had once used as a loaner unit. I took it out of the box, verified that it worked, and gave it to the lady the next day as a gift.

Something old in my garage was replaced by a grateful smile! Now that empty space in my garage reminds me that in giving, I actually create more space in my life.

Experience the magic of life
and you may find yourself speechless.

No Way To Say It

While doing a presentation one evening in 1996, I began to feel strongly affected by the message that was being expressed through me. When I finished, I couldn't speak. Someone came up and thanked me for what I said, and I wondered who they were speaking to.

Then a man approached and asked a question. I couldn't seem to answer him. Suddenly I saw myself at six or seven years old, looking at a book, unable to convert the abstract symbols we call words into something that felt real. I realized in that moment that words are no substitute for real life, and that what is essential cannot be spoken.

Again, the man asked his question. This time it was as if he was speaking to me from inside a glass bubble, and I was observing the event from everywhere at once. I could understand everything he asked, but couldn't understand *why he was asking.*

When we are in bliss, there are no questions and no answers. The heart is full and there is nothing to say. Fortunately the man understood, for I could barely speak the next few hours. I slipped into an indescribable state of peace, never to return the same again.

Enlightenment is seeing life as a gift.

If You Need, Please Take

It was a beautiful sunny day and I was out shopping with some friends in a quaint European town. The quiet cobblestone streets looked so inviting that I decided to sit on the sidewalk, close my eyes, and absorb the beauty of the afternoon. Sitting cross-legged with my baseball cap in my hands, I felt the warmth of the sun on my body, and floated away in a state of serenity. Suddenly, I had the feeling to open my eyes.

A man standing next to me was ready to drop some coins into my hat! Our eyes met and it became clear to him that I didn't need a donation, but he didn't know quite what to do. For a moment we just stared, then melted into each other's eyes until his conservative upbringing got the best of him, and he walked away embarrassed.

Once again I closed my eyes and slipped back into heaven. This time, however, I had a vision. I was sitting on the sidewalk in a state of bliss, with a sign and a large hat in front of me filled with money. The sign read, "If you need, please take."

Everything we experience
is part of our journey.
God makes no mistakes.

The Mystery of Life

If we have gained anything at all from our journey, it is to recognize that life is a mystery nobody understands. None of us knows how any of this happens, yet *life always takes us where we need to be.*

We sometimes like to think we are in charge—but we are not. We are just part of this big movie called life, and no matter what we do, we always get where we need to be! Whether the ride is smooth or bumpy has only to do with the journey our spirit is on …

And if we just stay present with it, everything eventually smooths out. Like an ocean after a storm, life becomes a still lake that gently lullabies us to sleep and whisks us away into the night.

Everything we do in life
is to get back to the place
we never left . . .
here.

Being Total

Right now an entirely new being is evolving that is neither male nor female. It is strong and sensitive, active and receptive, finely balanced, and exquisitely humane.

Up until now, we have divided our humanity so much to fit *our ideas* that we have robbed ourselves of our natural unity. Trying to be who we think we are "supposed" to be, we have forgotten that we are simply *human beings,* each on our own journey towards recovering wholeness.

This wholeness can only be regained by being total with everything we do, fully present and honest in each moment. If we love, we must love totally. If we share, we must share totally. We can no longer be part of anything that doesn't nourish our unity and our unconditional love for one another.

It is important for us now to merge into the oneness we have always been.

All minds
are an extension
of the One Mind.

Enlightenment

With presence, our awareness responds gracefully and spontaneously to life in each moment. We know that we are all One, so we draw no distinctions between ourselves.

We know that wisdom does not arise from the intellect, so we don't seek understanding through analysis or judgment.

We know that our greatest strength is our vulnerability, so we don't seek security or protection.

We see the Light, return to the Light, and become fully luminous *as the Light*.

Hidden Harmony

Imagine being in a state where nothing disturbs you, no matter what anyone says or does—where your mind doesn't judge or analyze, and you feel a deep love, caring, and connectedness with all of life. In this state, the observer and the observed are no longer separate. Everything you experience is both a mirror of your own consciousness and a window unto your own potential.

We all long for this kind of harmony in our lives, but rarely experience it for more than a fleeting moment. After years of looking, trying, and experimenting, one day when I *wasn't* looking, trying, and experimenting, I found myself in this magical state.

Now I feel moved to share this experience that my intellect cannot perceive and my words cannot express. Language alone cannot convey the heart of the spiritual journey, so profound yet so ordinary that when one is living it, there is no inner movement toward words. Trying to describe it only takes one out of this experience, yet sitting in silence doesn't share it either.

It is time to begin an uncharted journey, not knowing where we will end up. It is not only a journey into the unknown, but into the *unknowable*.

I'm hoping you will find this "hidden harmony" within yourself ...

There's nowhere to go ...
but if you keep showing up,
you'll arrive!

*A tremendous potential for self-discovery
lies within every moment of life,
if we could just stop and recognize it.*

Is There Any Moment But Now?

With every new scientific breakthrough, the worlds of quantum physics and metaphysics grow closer—another indication that the day is fast approaching when we will once again "see the Light."

As we look towards that day, it is important to recognize that it will come much faster *if we rise to meet it.* As the old saying goes, "When you take one step toward God, God takes ninety-nine steps toward you …"

We can begin ushering in this new era by practicing a more expansive way of being. This is neither a scientific nor spiritual philosophy, but simply a way of living and relating that is accessible to anyone who wishes to unite joyfully with life *in each moment.*

Mystics seek the meaning of life in meditation, and physicists pursue the same end with equations and experiments—and the everyday person, who is neither seer nor scientist, *also* has a means of discovering the secrets of life, health, and happiness.

The Beginning…